HAL•LEONARD®
GUITAR
PLAY-ALONG

PINK FLOYD
CLASSICS

AUDIO
ACCESS
INCLUDED

PLAYBACK+
Speed • Pitch • Balance • Loop

To access audio visit:
www.halleonard.com/mylibrary

Enter Code
4647-8433-8052-4071

Cover photo © Jean-Claude Deutsch/Getty Images

ISBN: 978-1-4950-2266-1

In Australia Contact:
Hal Leonard Australia Pty. Ltd.
4 Lentara Court
Cheltenham, Victoria, 3192 Australia
Email: ausadmin@halleonard.com.au

For all works contained herein:
Unauthorized copying, arranging, adapting, recording, Internet posting,
public performance, or other distribution of the printed or recorded
music in this publication is an infringement of copyright.
Infringers are liable under the law.

Visit Hal Leonard Online at **www.halleonard.com**

HAL•LEONARD®

7777 W. BLUEMOUND RD. P.O. BOX 13819
MILWAUKEE, WISCONSIN 53213

C000142580

CONTENTS

Guitar Notation Legend

THE MUSICAL STAFF shows pitches and rhythms and is divided by bar lines into measures. Pitches are named after the first seven letters of the alphabet.

TABLATURE graphically represents the guitar fingerboard. Each horizontal line represents a string, and each number represents a fret.

Notes:

Strings:
high E
B
G
D
A
low E

4th string, 2nd fret   1st & 2nd strings open, played together   open D chord

HALF-STEP BEND: Strike the note and bend up 1/2 step.

WHOLE-STEP BEND: Strike the note and bend up one step.

GRACE NOTE BEND: Strike the note and immediately bend up as indicated.

SLIGHT (MICROTONE) BEND: Strike the note and bend up 1/4 step.

BEND AND RELEASE: Strike the note and bend up as indicated, then release back to the original note. Only the first note is struck.

PRE-BEND: Bend the note as indicated, then strike it.

VIBRATO: The string is vibrated by rapidly bending and releasing the note with the fretting hand.

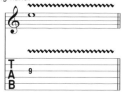

PALM MUTING: The note is partially muted by the pick hand lightly touching the string(s) just before the bridge.

HAMMER-ON: Strike the first (lower) note with one finger, then sound the higher note (on the same string) with another finger by fretting it without picking.

PULL-OFF: Place both fingers on the notes to be sounded. Strike the first note and without picking, pull the finger off to sound the second (lower) note.

LEGATO SLIDE: Strike the first note and then slide the same fret-hand finger up or down to the second note. The second note is not struck.

SHIFT SLIDE: Same as legato slide, except the second note is struck.

TRILL: Very rapidly alternate between the notes indicated by continuously hammering on and pulling off.

TAPPING: Hammer ("tap") the fret indicated with the pick-hand index or middle finger and pull off to the note fretted by the fret hand.

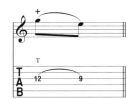

NATURAL HARMONIC: Strike the note while the fret-hand lightly touches the string directly over the fret indicated.

PINCH HARMONIC: The note is fretted normally and a harmonic is produced by adding the edge of the thumb or the tip of the index finger of the pick hand to the normal pick attack.

TREMOLO PICKING: The note is picked as rapidly and continuously as possible.

VIBRATO BAR DIVE AND RETURN: The pitch of the note or chord is dropped a specified number of steps (in rhythm), then returned to the original pitch.

VIBRATO BAR SCOOP: Depress the bar just before striking the note, then quickly release the bar.

VIBRATO BAR DIP: Strike the note and then immediately drop a specified number of steps, then release back to the original pitch.

Additional Musical Definitions

    (accent)   • Accentuate note (play it louder).

    (staccato)   • Play the note short.

D.S. al Coda   • Go back to the sign (%), then play until the measure marked "*To Coda*," then skip to the section labelled "**Coda**."

D.C. al Fine   • Go back to the beginning of the song and play until the measure marked "***Fine***" (end).

Fill   • Label used to identify a brief melodic figure which is to be inserted into the arrangement.

N.C.   • Harmony is implied.

• Repeat measures between signs.

• When a repeated section has different endings, play the first ending only the first time and the second ending only the second time.

Another Brick in the Wall, Part 2

Words and Music by Roger Waters

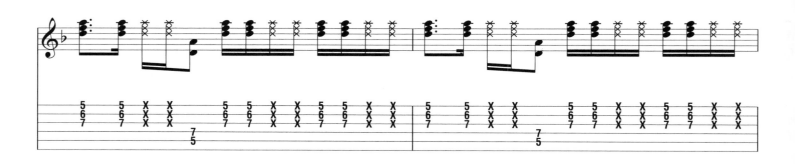

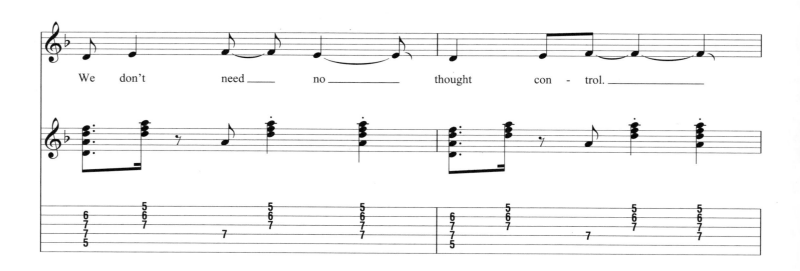

Copyright © 1979 Roger Waters Music Overseas Ltd.
All Rights Administered by BMG Rights Management (US) LLC
All Rights Reserved   Used by Permission

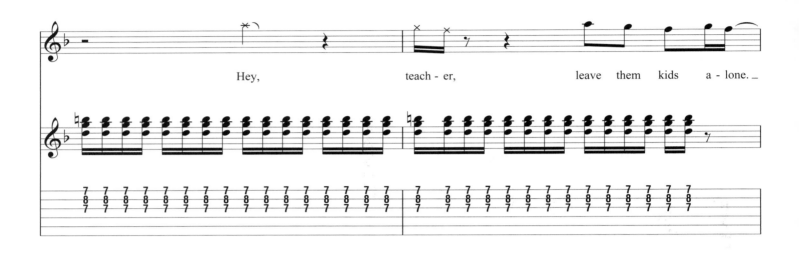

Hey, teach-er, leave them kids a-lone.

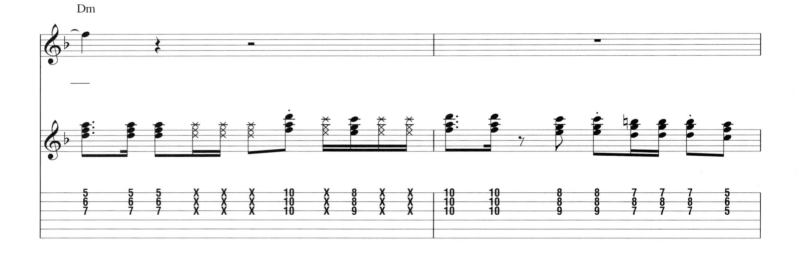

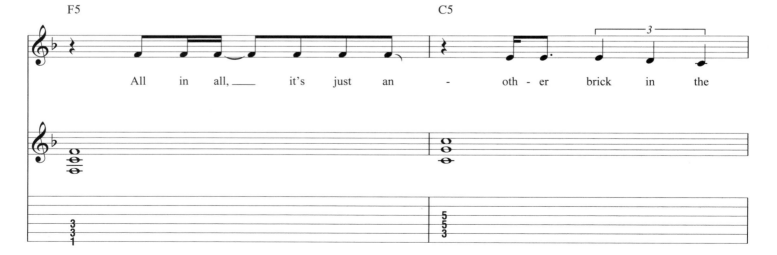

All in all, ___ it's just an-oth-er brick in the

We don't need ___ no ___ thought con - trol. ___

No dark sar - cas ___ m ___ in the class - room.

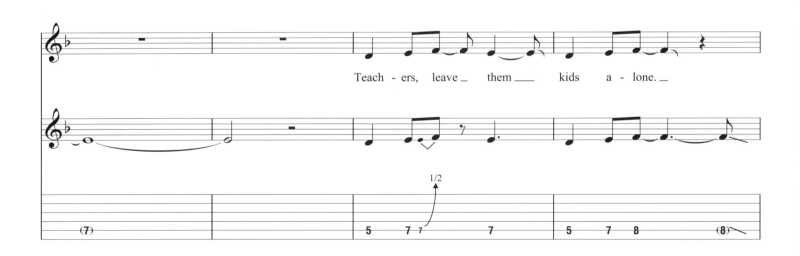

Teach - ers, leave ___ them ___ kids a - lone. ___

G

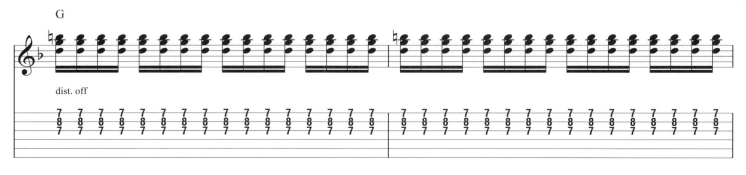

dist. off

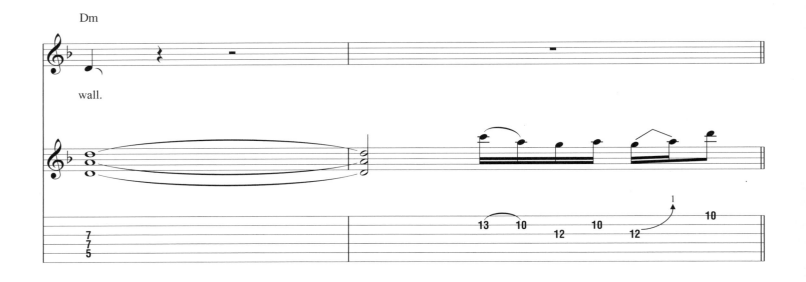

Guitar Solo

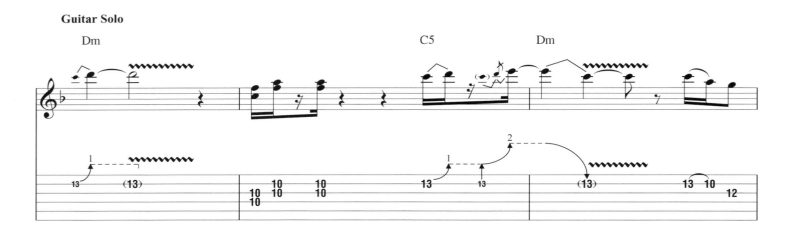

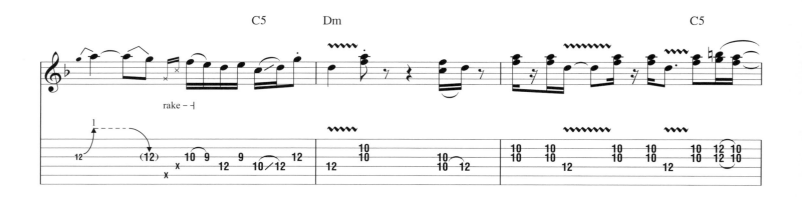

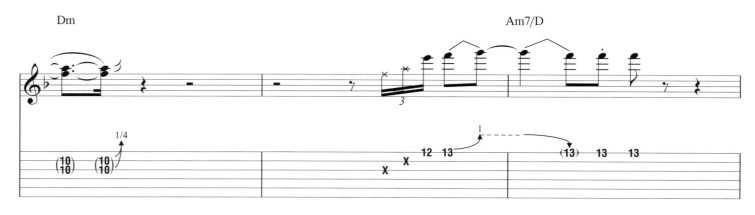

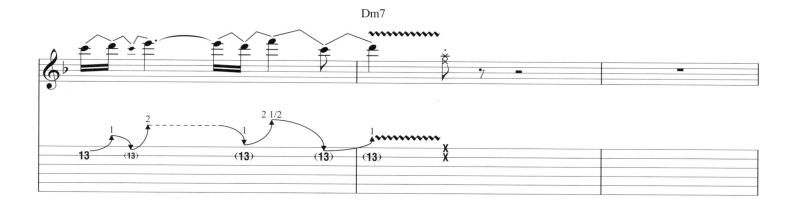

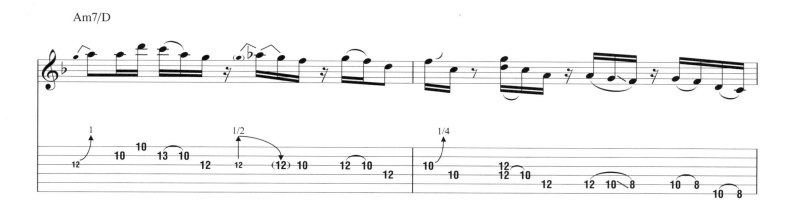

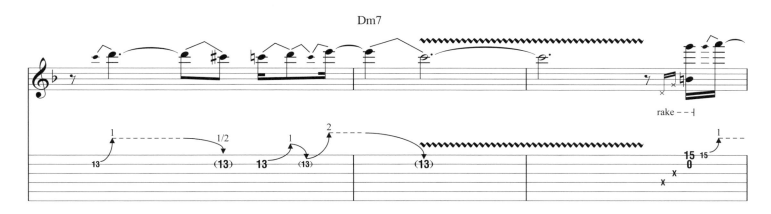

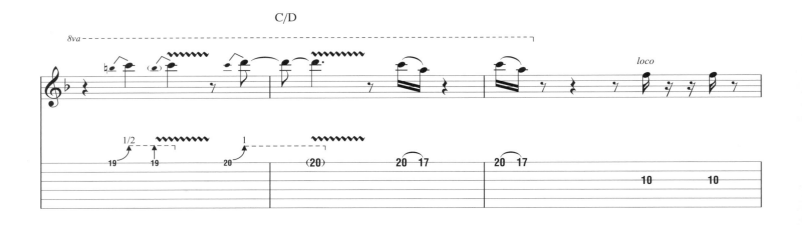

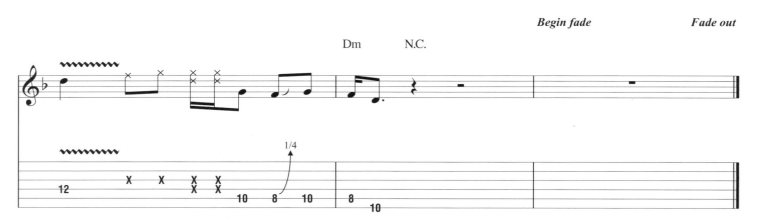

Mother

Words and Music by Roger Waters

Copyright © 1979 Roger Waters Music Overseas Ltd.
All Rights Administered by BMG Rights Management (US) LLC
All Rights Reserved   Used by Permission

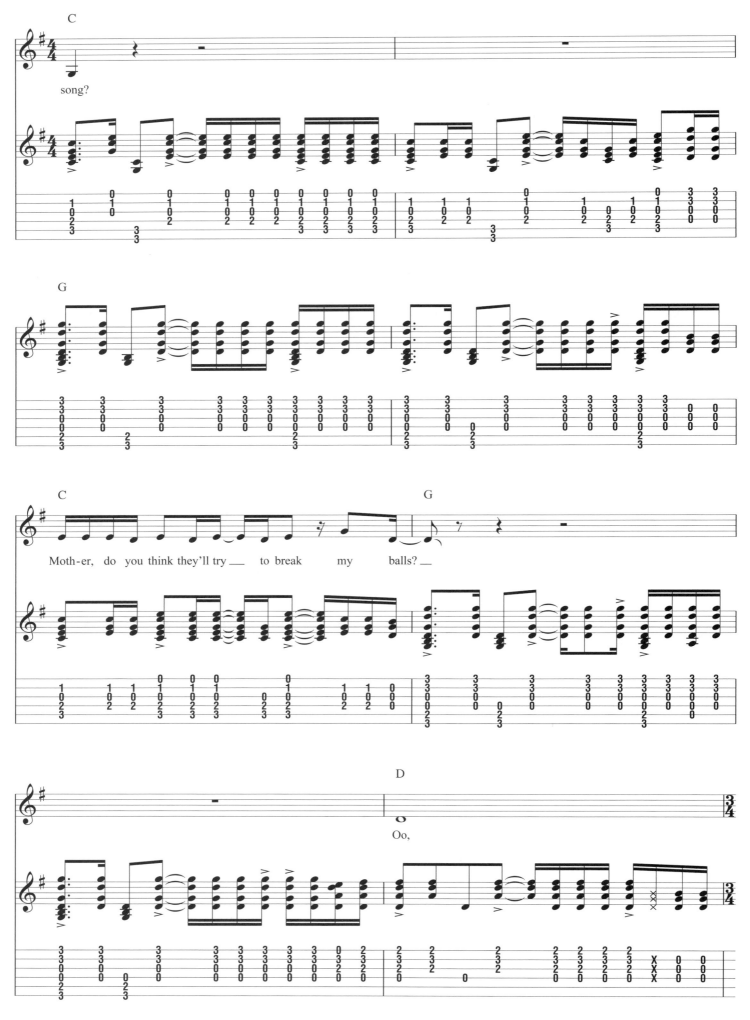

song?

Moth-er, do you think they'll try ___ to break ___ my ___ balls? ___

Oo,

ah. Moth - er, should I build the wall? ____

℅ **Verse**

2. Moth - er, should I run   for   pres - i -
3. *See additional lyrics*

dent?

Moth - er, should I trust the gov - ern - ment? ____

Moth - er, will they put me in ____ the fir - ing

line?

To Coda ⊕

co - zy and warm.

Oo, babe.

Oo, babe.

Oo, babe, of course Ma - ma's gon - na help build the wall.

w/ dist.

Guitar Solo

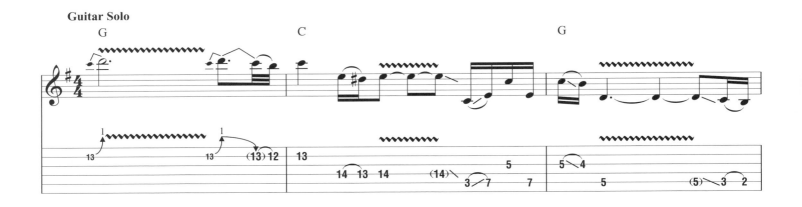

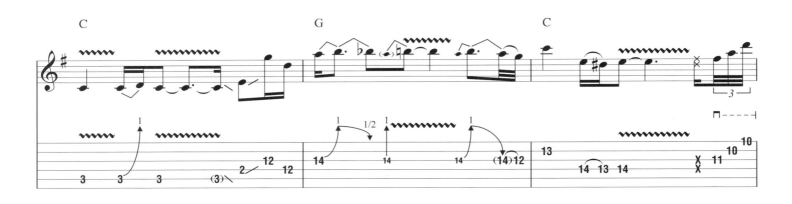

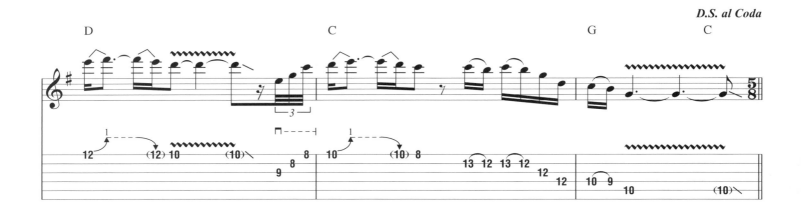

D.S. al Coda

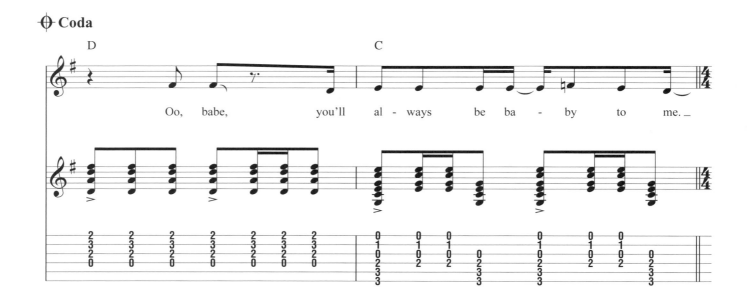

Oo, babe, you'll al - ways be ba - by to me.

Outro

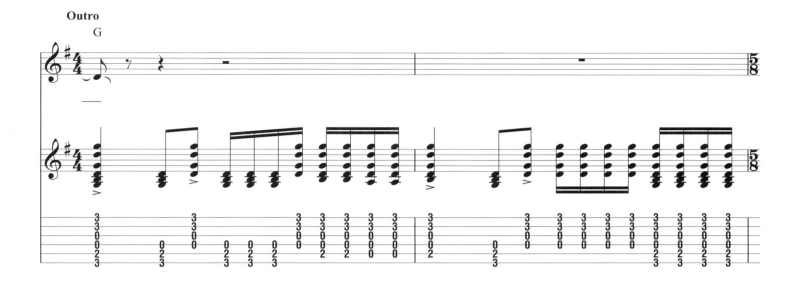

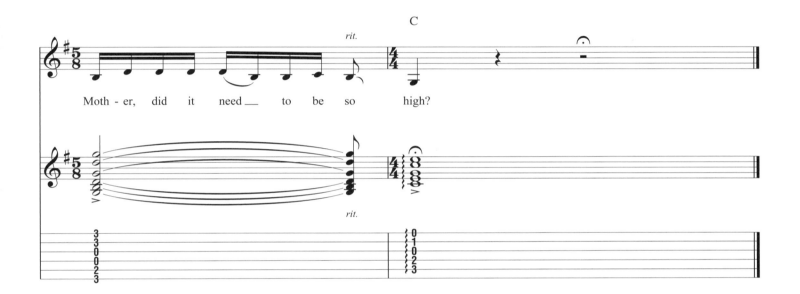

Moth - er, did it need _ to be so high?

Additional Lyrics

3. Mother, do you think she's good enough
   For me?
   Mother, do you think she's dangerous
   To me?
   Mother, will she tear your little boy apart?
   Oo, ah. Mother, will she break my heart?

Chorus Hush now, baby, baby, don't you cry.
   Mama's gonna check out all your girlfriends for you.
   Mama won't let anyone dirty get through.
   Mama's gonna wait up until you get in.
   Mama will always find out where you've been.
   Mama's gonna keep baby healthy and clean.
   Oo, babe. Oo, babe.
   Oo, babe, you'll always be baby to me.

Comfortably Numb

Words and Music by Roger Waters and David Gilmour

Copyright © 1979 Roger Waters Music Overseas Ltd. and Pink Floyd Music Publishers, Inc.
All Rights for Roger Waters Music Overseas Ltd. Administered by BMG Rights Management (US) LLC
All Rights Reserved   Used by Permission

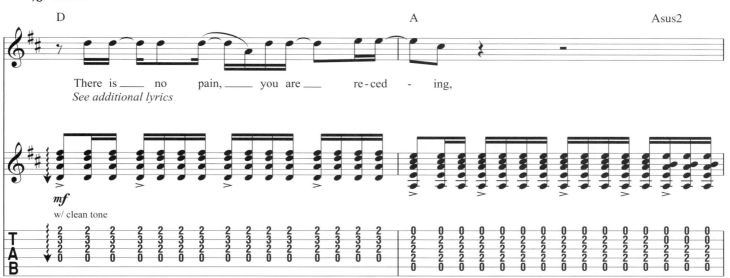

There is __ no pain, __ you are __ re - ced - ing,
See additional lyrics

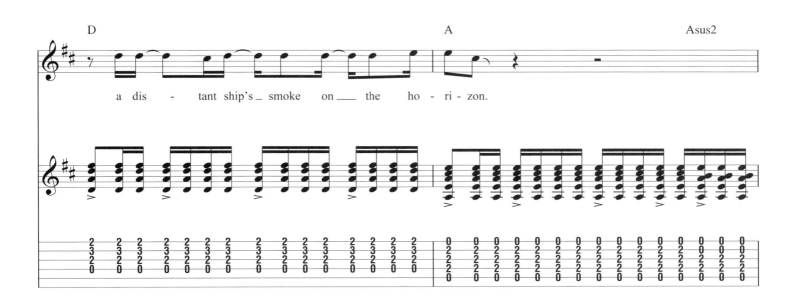

a dis - tant ship's _ smoke on __ the ho - ri - zon.

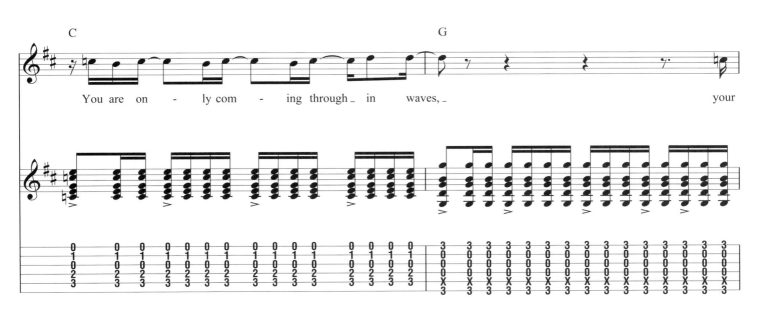

You are on - ly com - ing through _ in waves, _ your

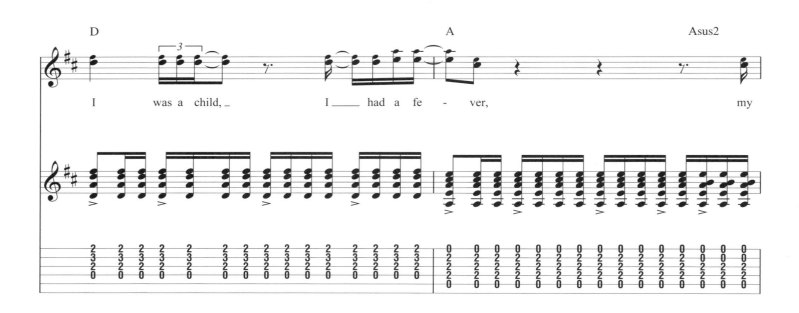

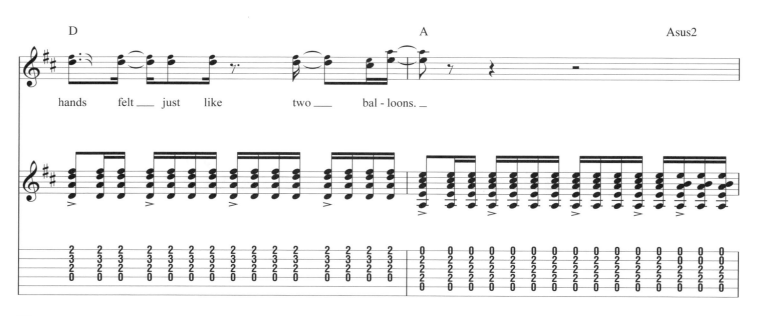

26

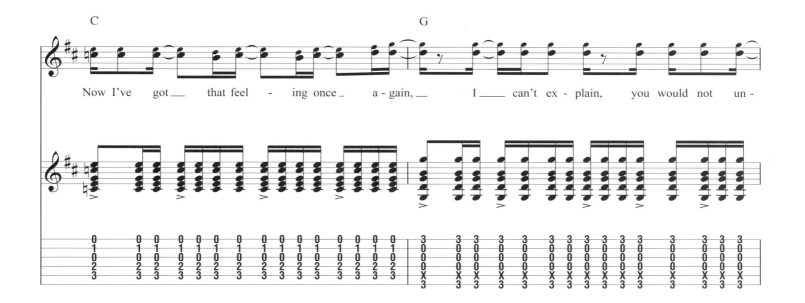

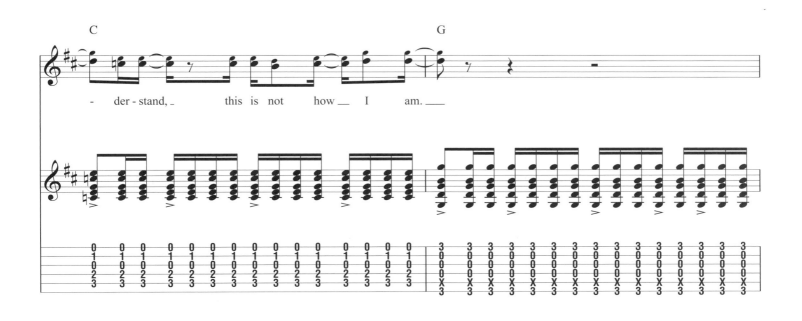

To Coda ⊕

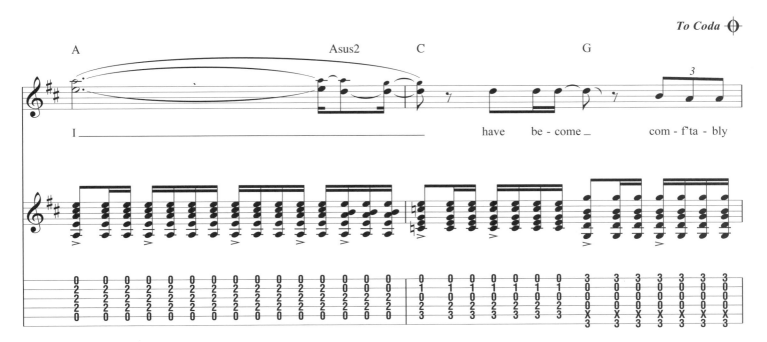

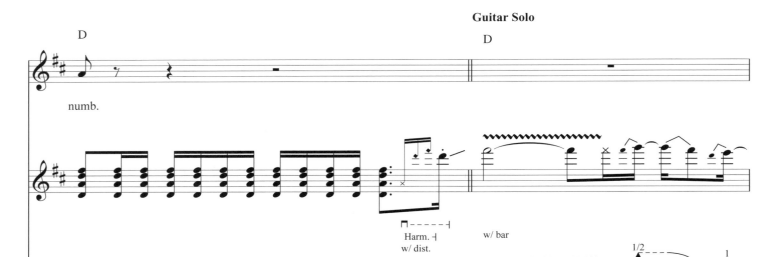

numb.

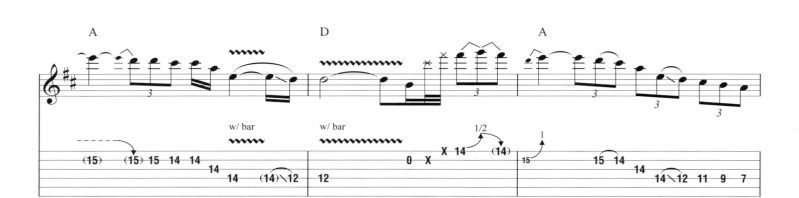

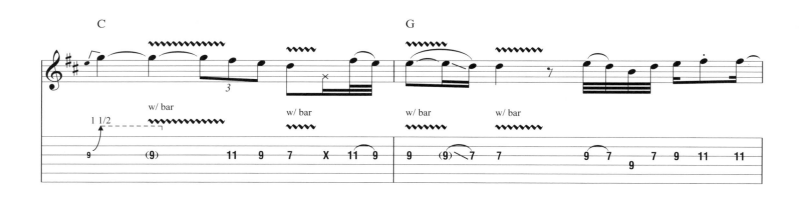

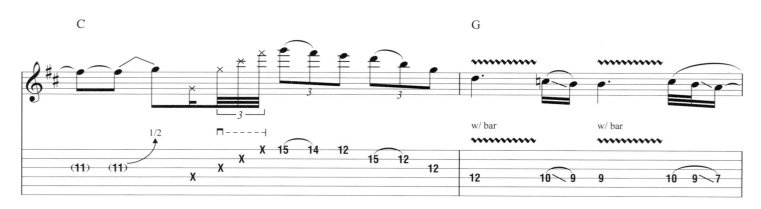

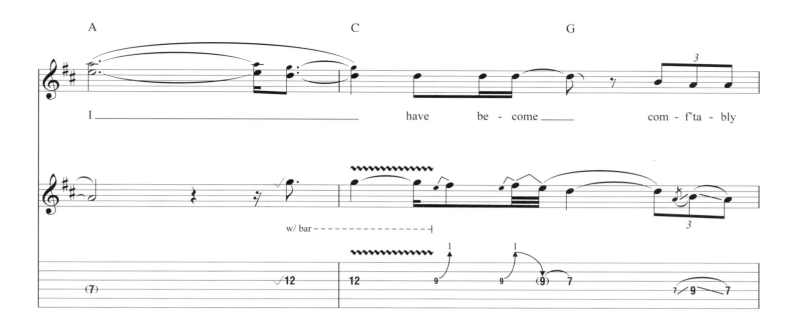

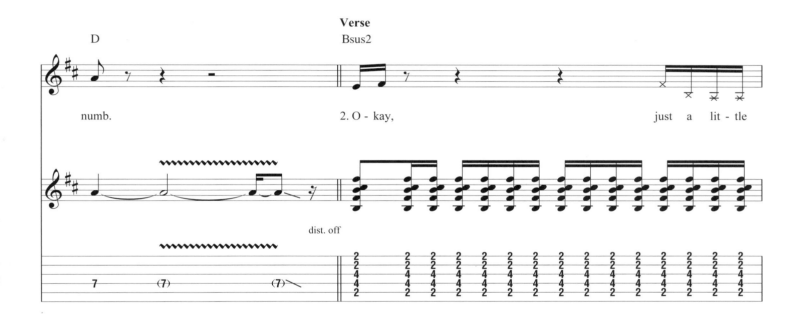

Verse

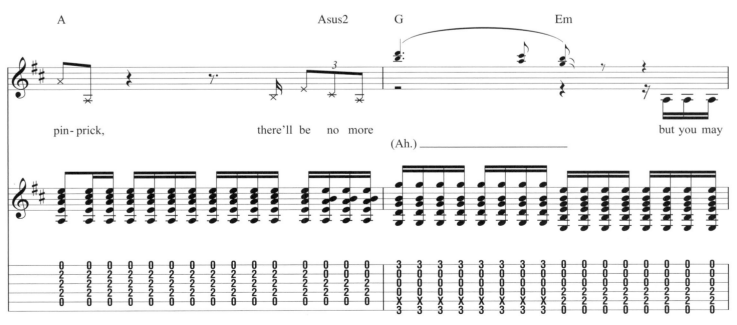

feel a lit - tle sick. Can you stand up? I do be - lieve it's

work - ing, good, that - 'll keep you go - ing through the show, come

D.S. al Coda

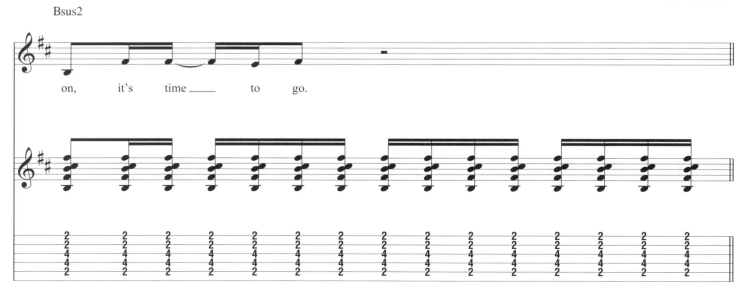

on, it's time ____ to go.

⊕ Coda

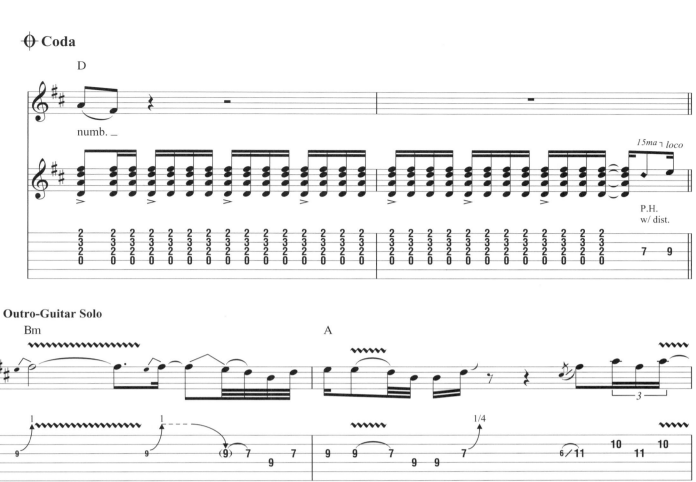

numb.

15ma ⌐ loco

P.H.
w/ dist.

Outro-Guitar Solo

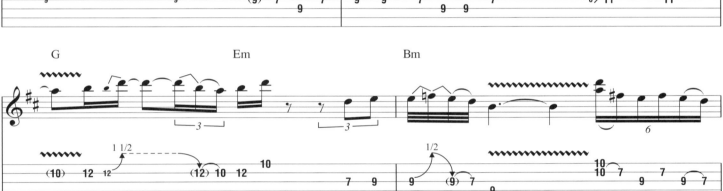

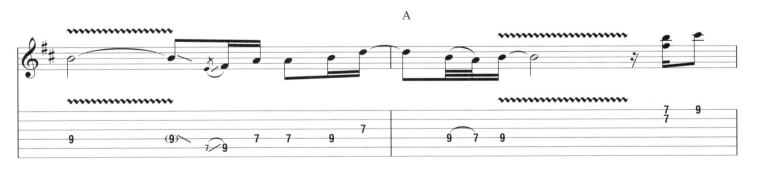

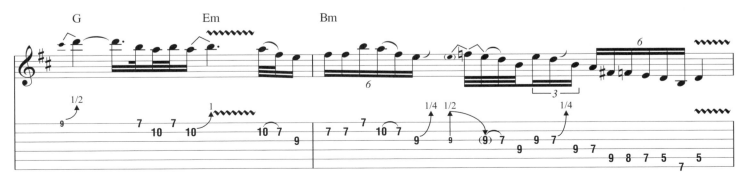

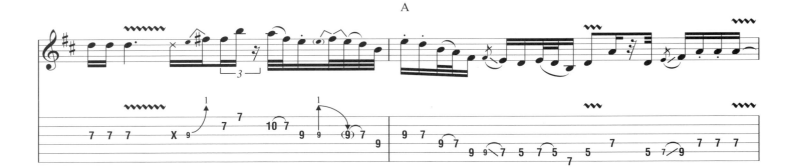

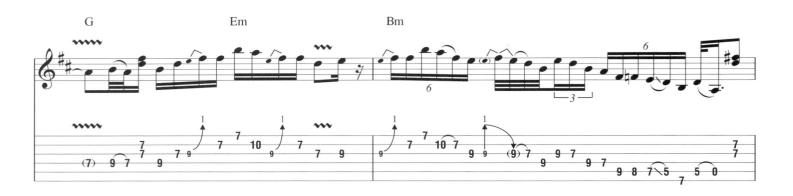

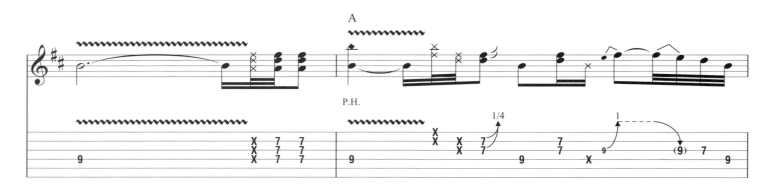

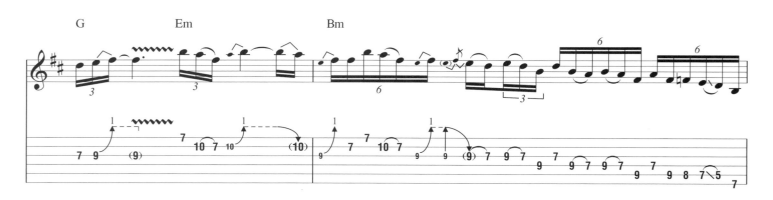

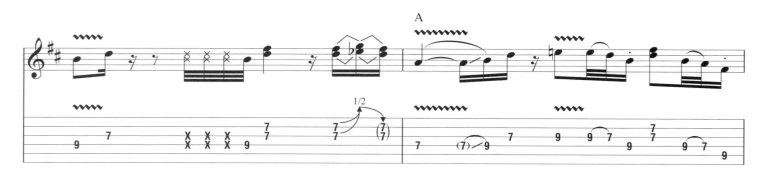

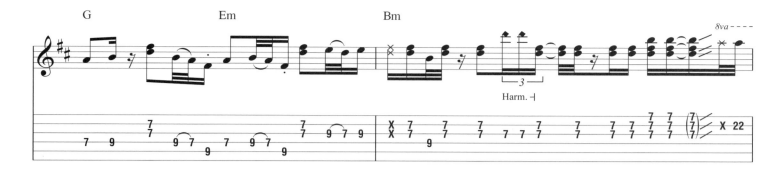

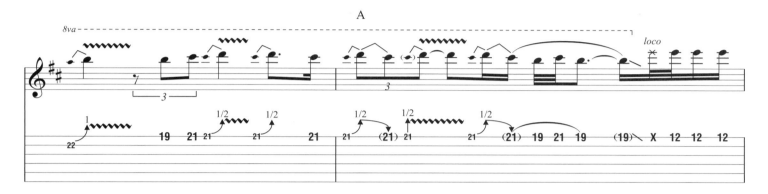

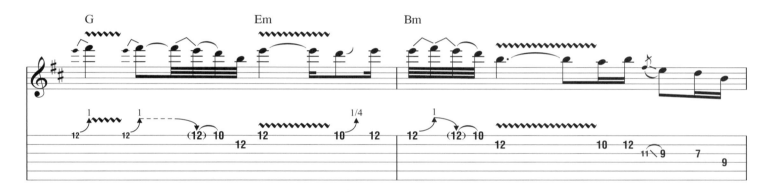

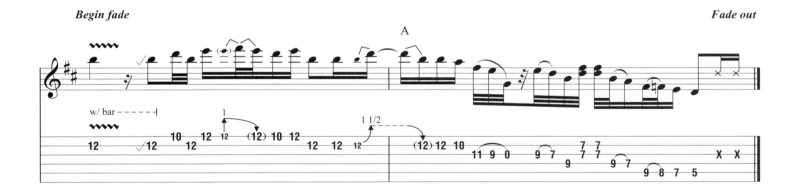

Additional Lyrics

Chorus   There is no pain, you are receding,
A distant ship's smoke on the horizon.
You are only coming through in waves.
Your lips move, but I can't hear what you're saying.
When I was a child, I caught a fleeting glimpse
Out of the corner of my eye.
I turned to look but it was gone.
I cannot put my finger on it now;
The child has grown, the dream is gone.
I have become comf'tably numb.

Goodbye Blue Sky

Words and Music by Roger Waters

(Birds chirping & airplane)

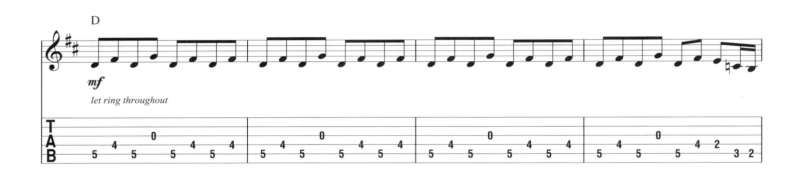

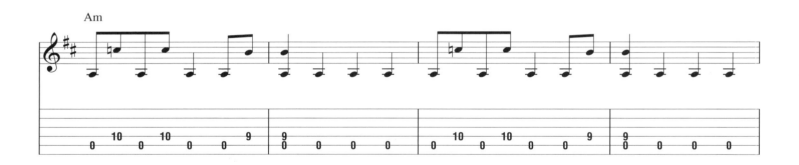

Copyright © 1979 Roger Waters Music Overseas Ltd.
All Rights Administered by BMG Rights Management (US) LLC
All Rights Reserved   Used by Permission

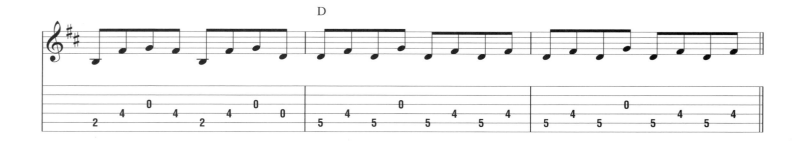

Interlude

Oo.

Verse

2. Did, did, did, did you see the fright-ened ones? Did, did, did, did you hear the fall-ing bombs?

The flames are all long gone, but the pain lin-gers on.

Chorus

Good - bye, blue __ sky, __ good - bye, __ blue ____ sky, __ good - bye, __

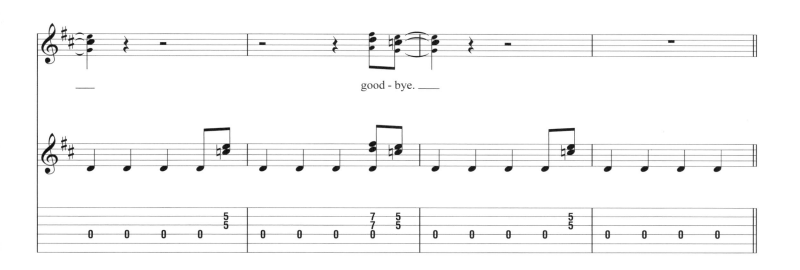

__ good - bye. ____

Outro

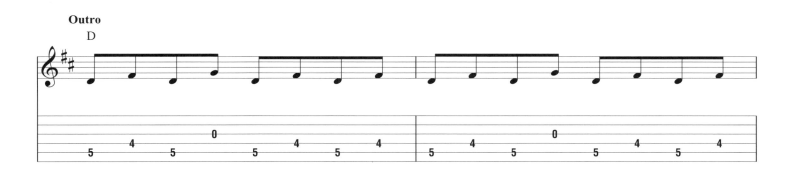

Begin fade   *Fade out*

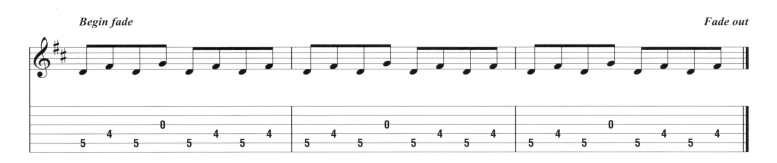

37

Hey You

Words and Music by Roger Waters

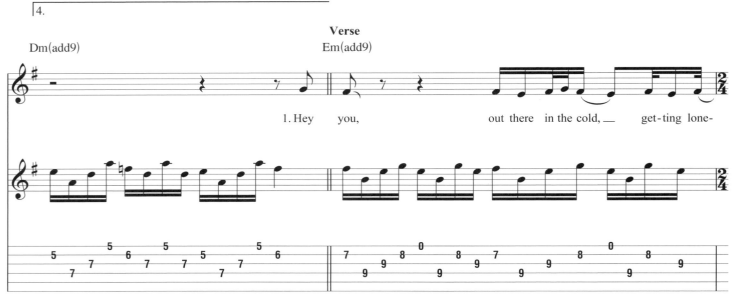

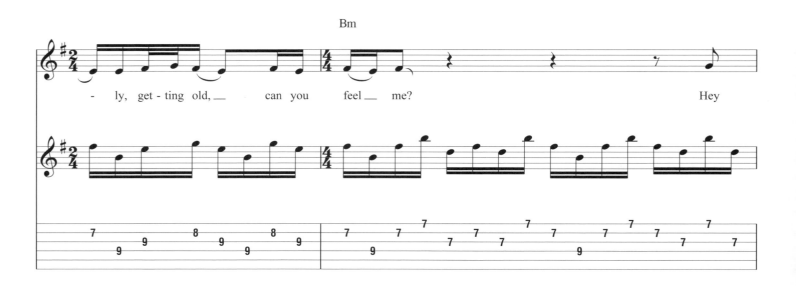

Copyright © 1979 Roger Waters Music Overseas Ltd.
All Rights Administered by BMG Rights Management (US) LLC
All Rights Reserved   Used by Permission

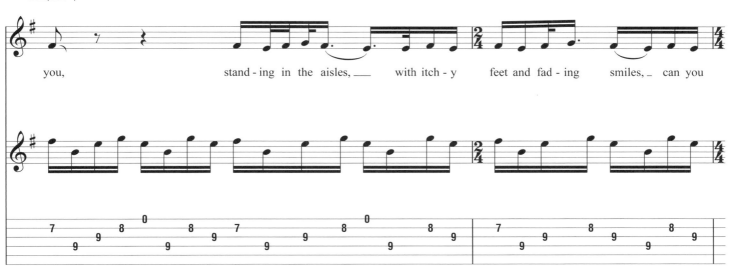

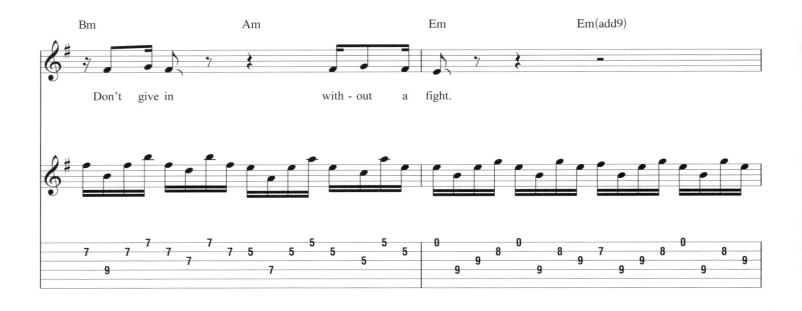

Verse

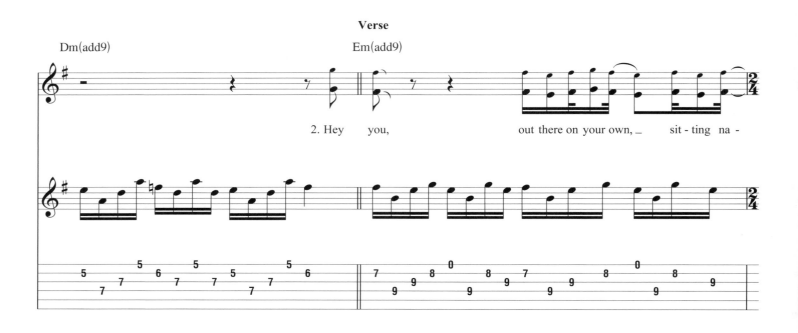

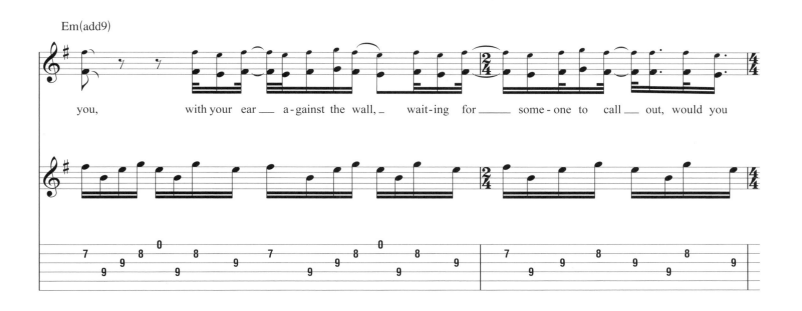

you, with your ear — a-gainst the wall, — wait-ing for ——— some-one to call — out, would you

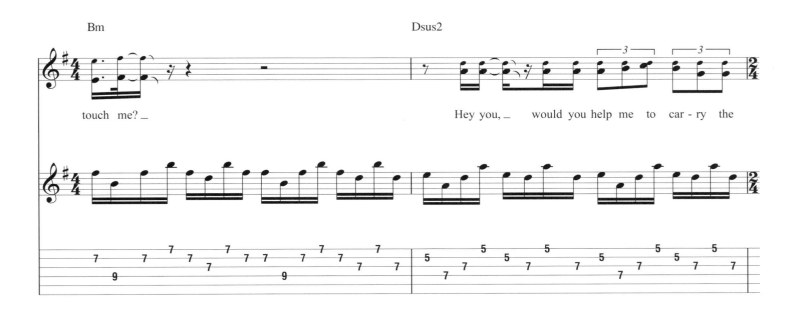

touch me? — Hey you, — would you help me to car-ry the

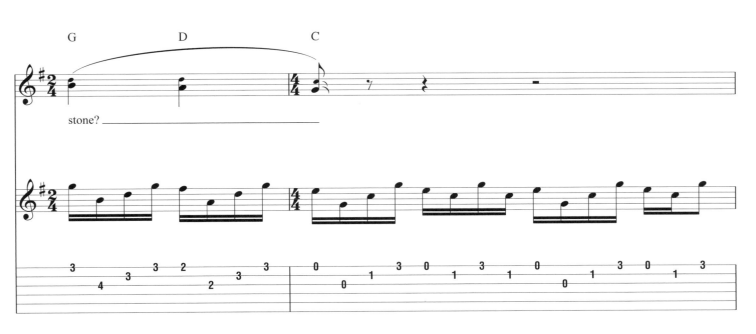

stone? _____

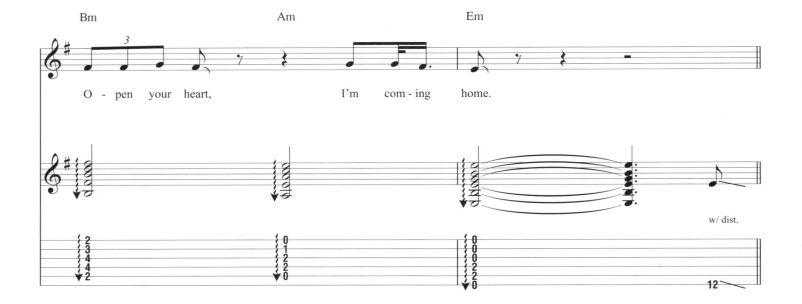

O - pen your heart, I'm com - ing home.

Guitar Solo

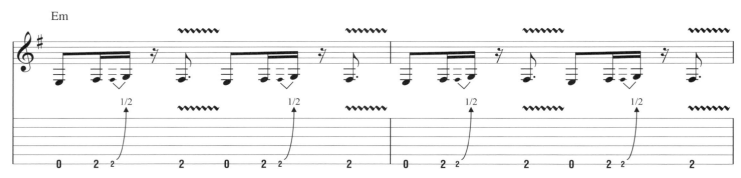

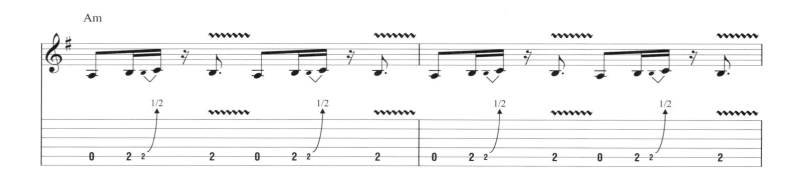

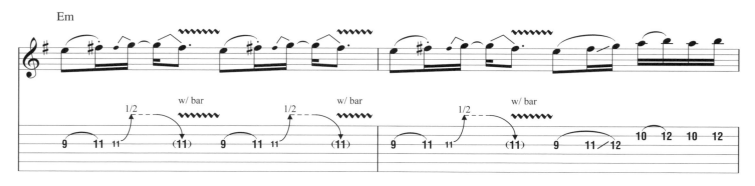

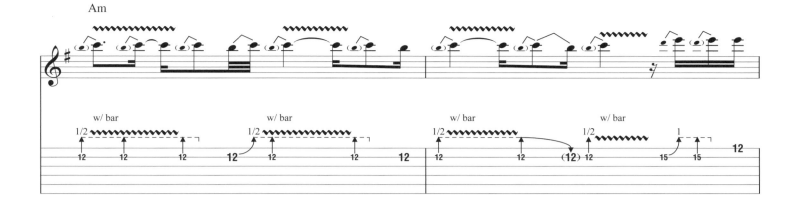

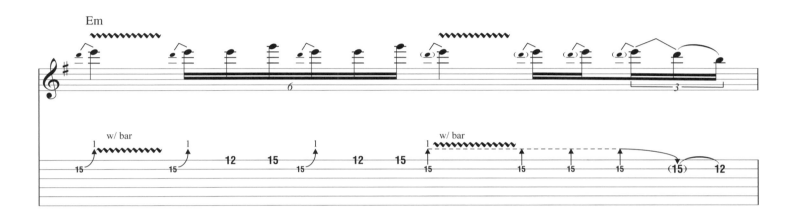

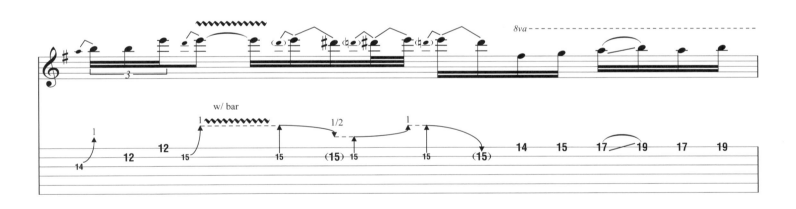

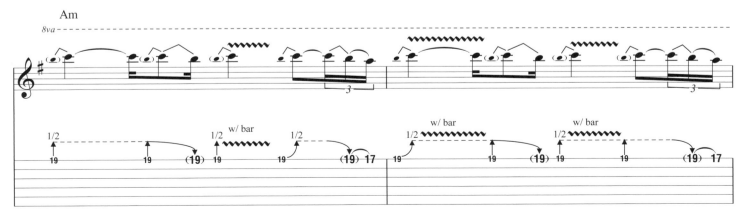

Bridge

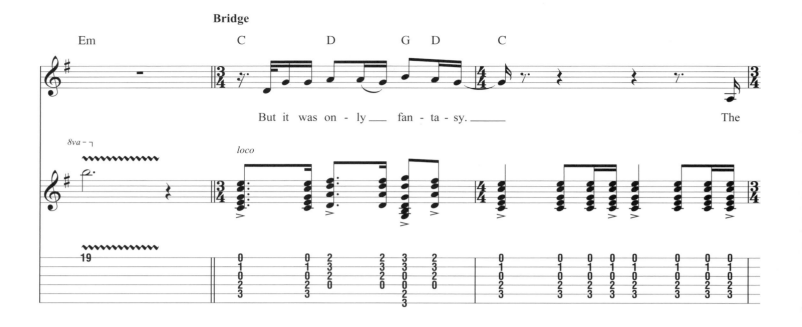

But it was on - ly ___ fan - ta - sy. ___ The

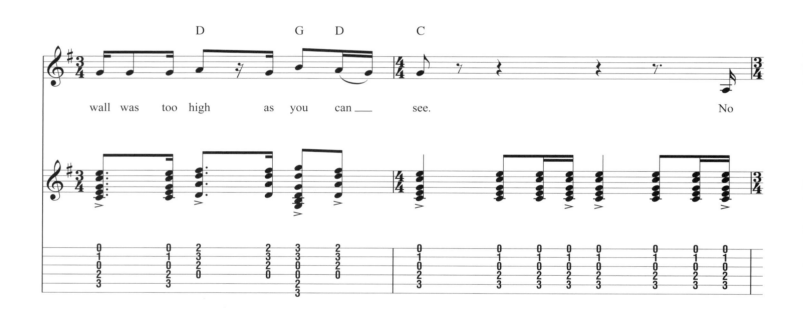

wall was too high as you can ___ see. No

mat - ter how he tried ___ he could not break free. And the

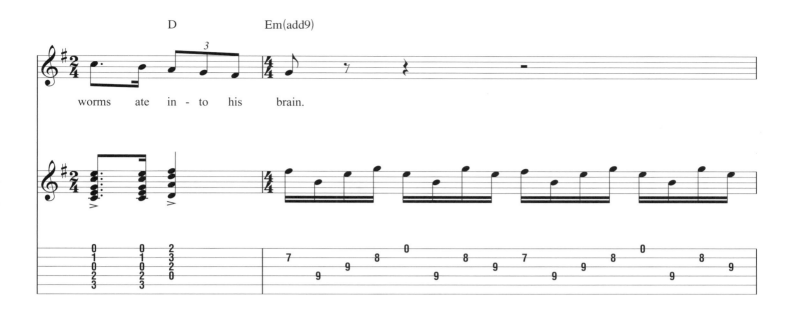

worms   ate   in - to   his   brain.

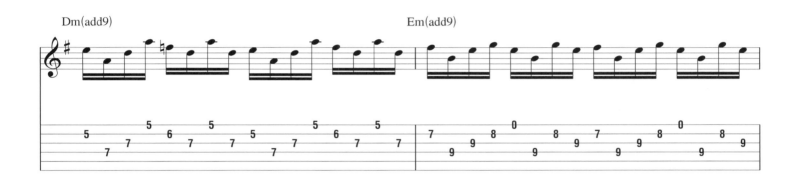

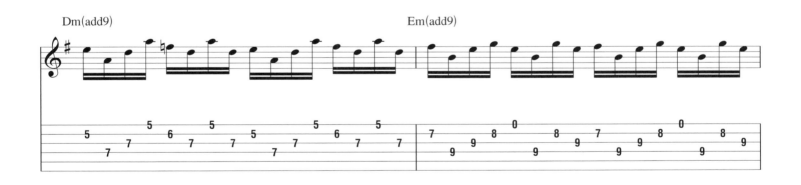

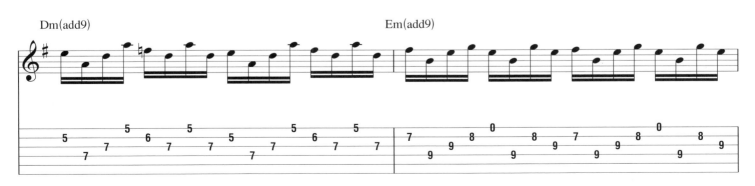

Verse

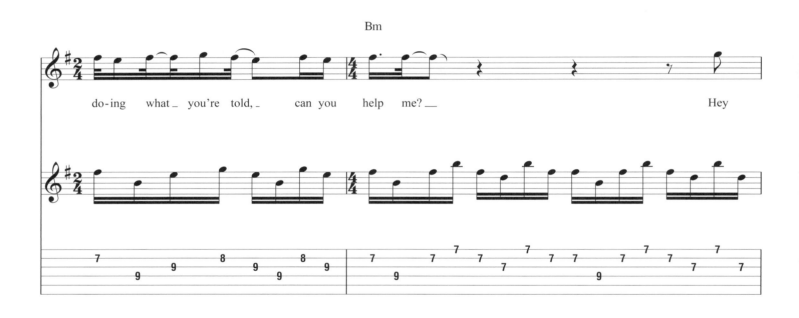

46

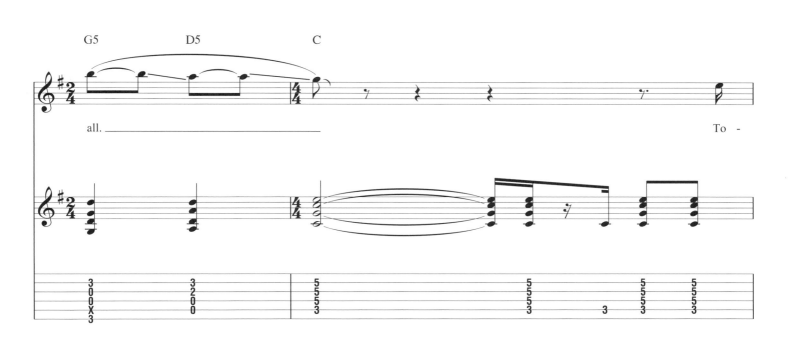

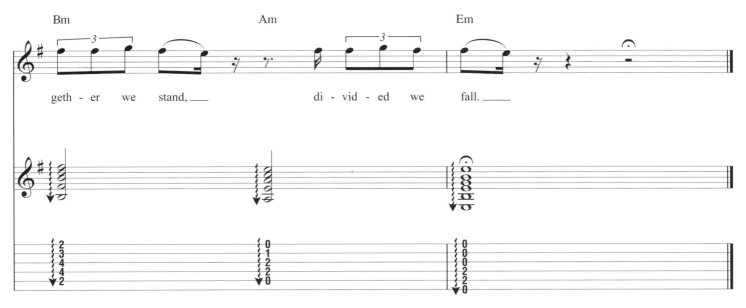

Welcome to the Machine

Words and Music by Roger Waters

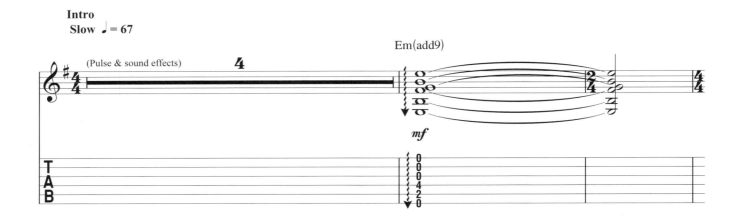

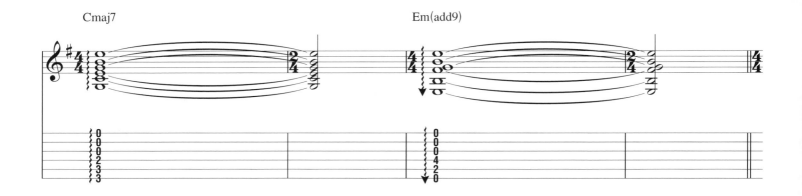

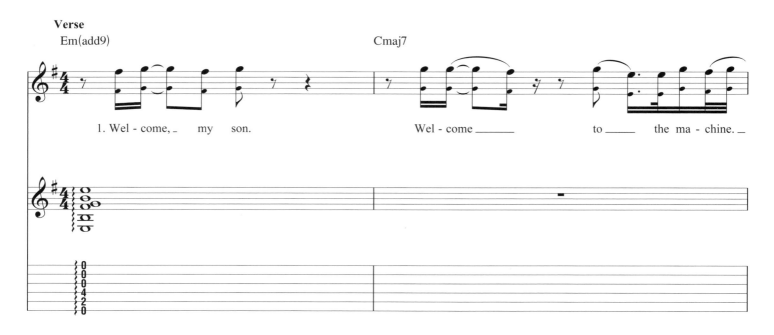

Copyright © 1975 Roger Waters Music Overseas Ltd.
Copyright Renewed
All Rights Administered by BMG Rights Management (US) LLC
All Rights Reserved   Used by Permission

Where have _ you been?

It's al - right, we know ___ where _ you've been.

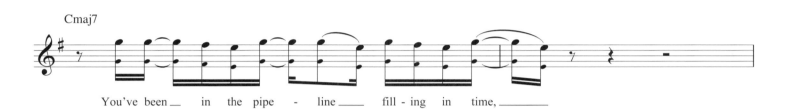

You've been ___ in the pipe - line ____ fill - ing in time, _____

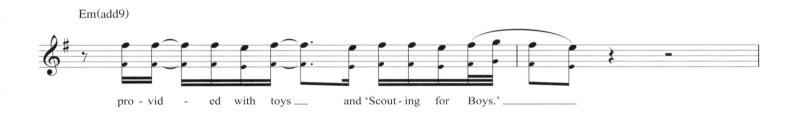

pro - vid - ed with toys ___ and 'Scout - ing for Boys.' _____

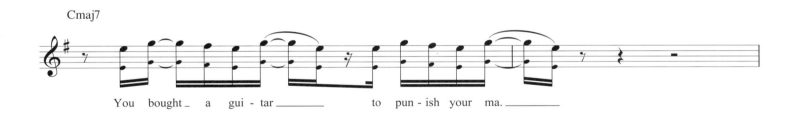

You bought _ a gui - tar _____ to pun - ish your ma. _____

You did - n't like school, _ and you know you're no - bod - y's fool. ____

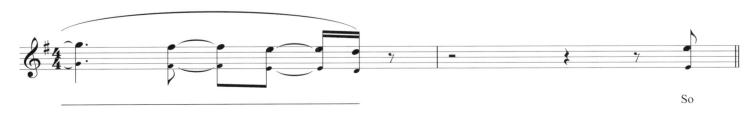

So

Interlude

To Coda ⊕

Em(add9)

Cmaj7　　　　　　　　**Em(add9)**　　　　　　　**Cmaj7**

D.S. al Coda　　　　⊕ **Coda**

Em(add9)

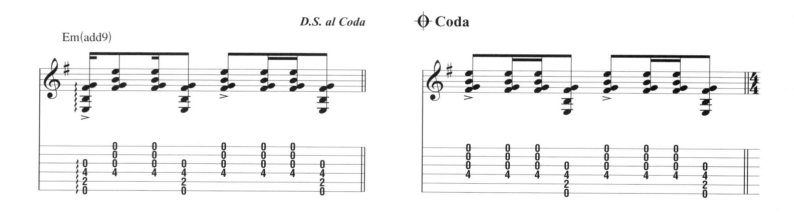

Verse

　Em　　　　　　　　　　　　　　　　　**C**

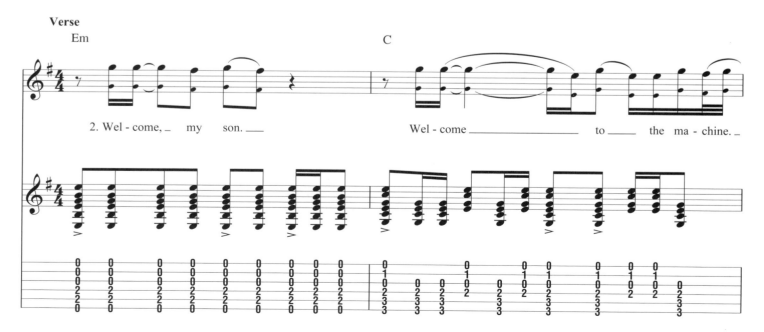

2. Wel - come, __ my son. __　　　　　Wel - come _____ to ____ the ma - chine. __

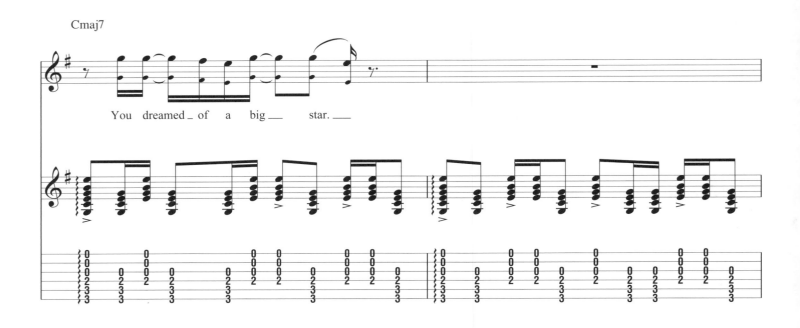

Cmaj7

You dreamed _ of _ a big ___ star. ___

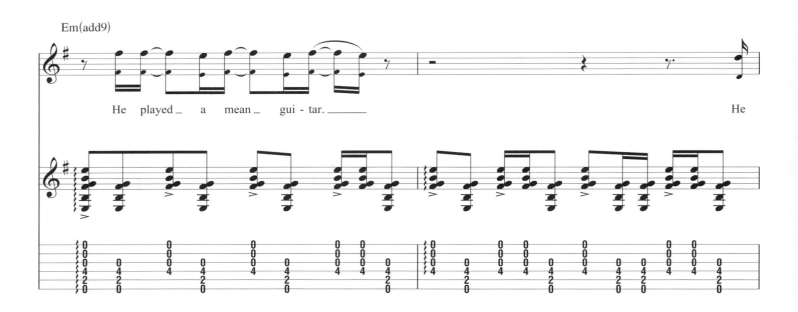

Em(add9)

He played _ a mean _ gui - tar. ___ He

Cmaj7

al - ways ate ___ at the Steak _ Bar. ___ He

loved to drive _ in his Jag - u - ar. _____ So

Chorus

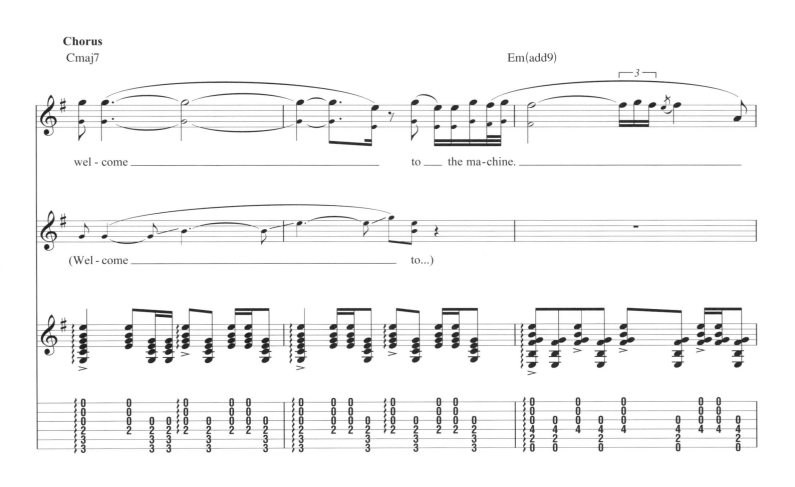

wel - come _____ to _____ the ma-chine.

(Wel - come _____ to...)

Repeat and fade

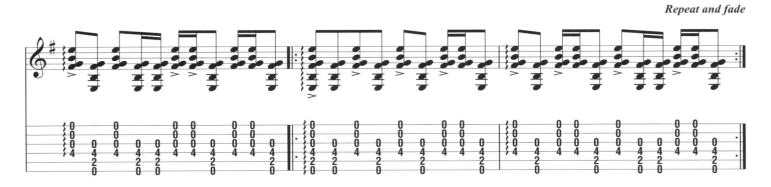

Wish You Were Here

Words and Music by Roger Waters and David Gilmour

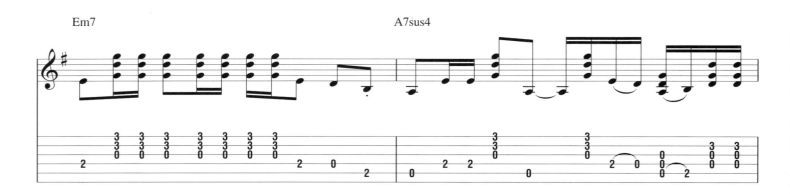

Copyright © 1975 Roger Waters Music Overseas Ltd. and Pink Floyd Music Publishers, Inc.
Copyright Renewed
All Rights for Roger Waters Music Overseas Ltd. Administered by BMG Rights Management (US) LLC
All Rights Reserved   Used by Permission

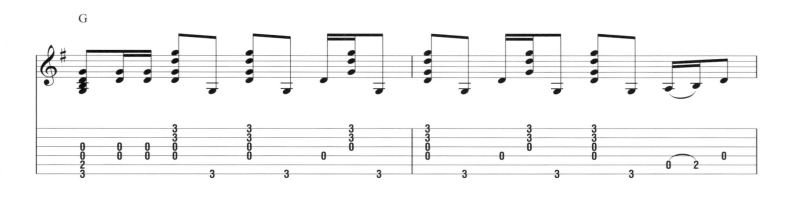

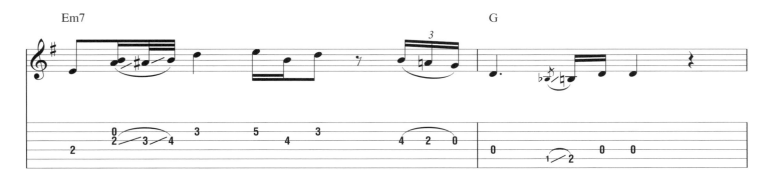

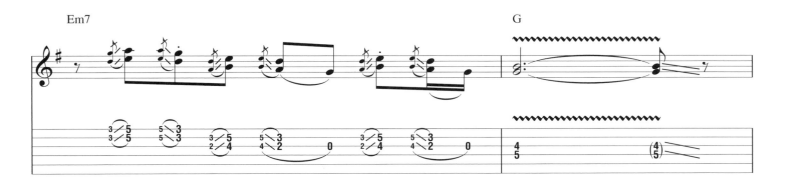

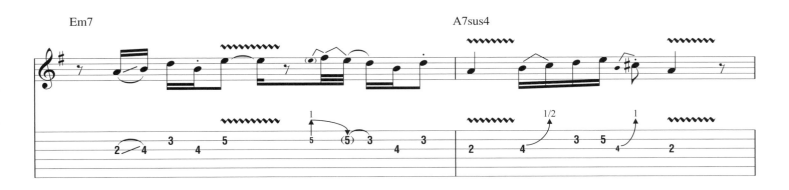

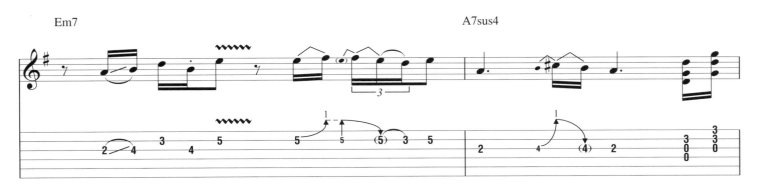

Verse

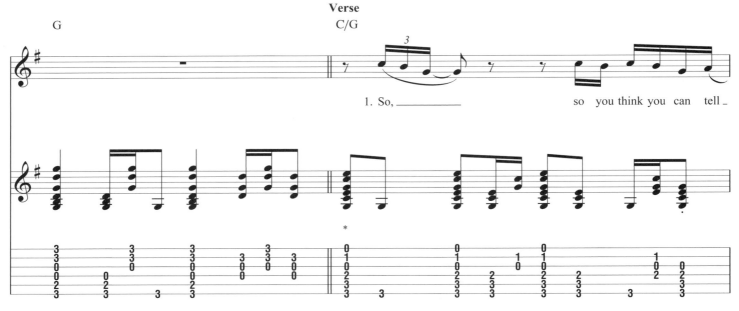

1. So, _____ so you think you can tell ___

*P.M. 6th, 5th & 4th strings, next 7 1/2 meas.

___ heav - en from hell, _____ blue skies ___ from pain. ___

___ Can you tell a green field _____ from a cold _____ steel

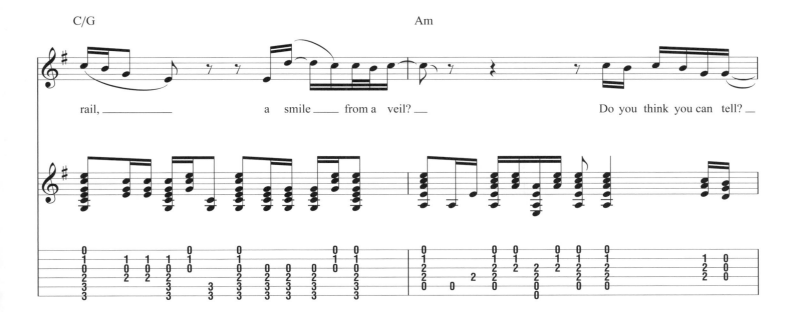

rail, _____ a smile _____ from a veil? _____ Do you think you can tell? _

_____ Did they get you to trade _____ your he - roes for

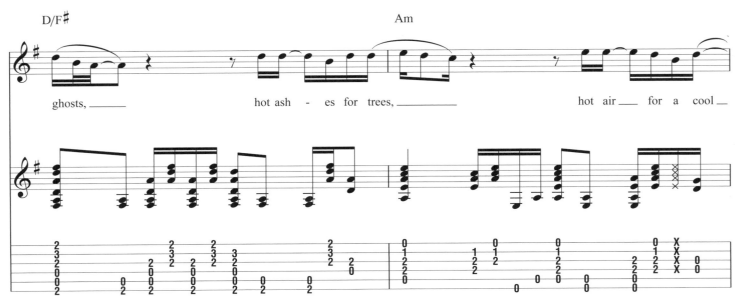

ghosts, _____ hot ash - es for trees, _____ hot air _____ for a cool _____

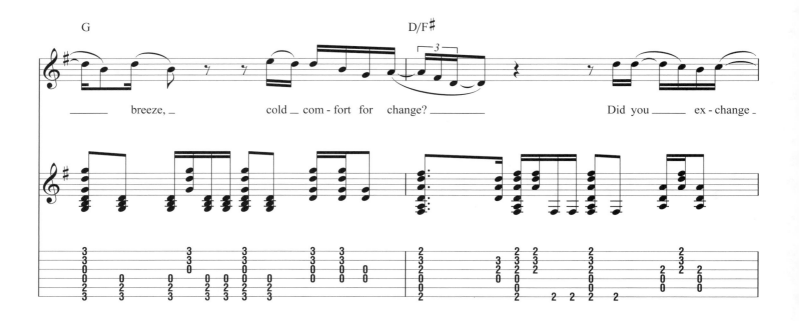

breeze, _ cold _ com-fort for change? _____ Did you _____ ex-change _

_____ a walk-on part _ in the war ____ for a lead _____ role in a cage? __

Guitar Solo

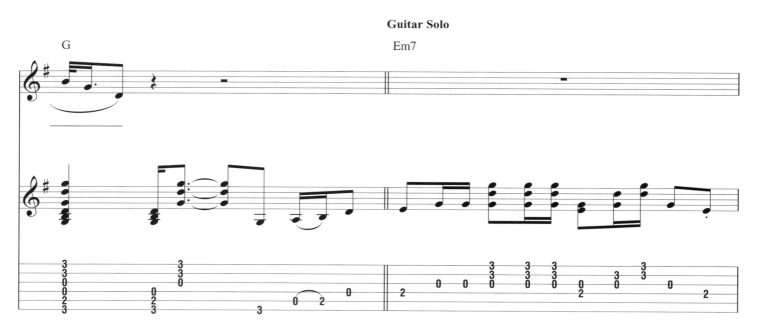

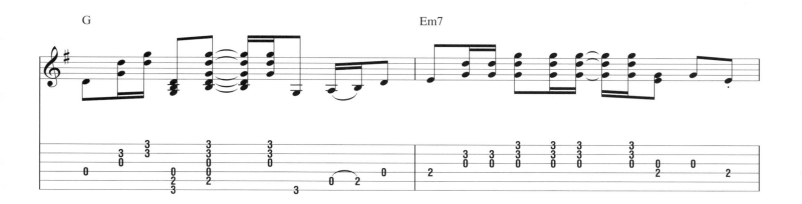

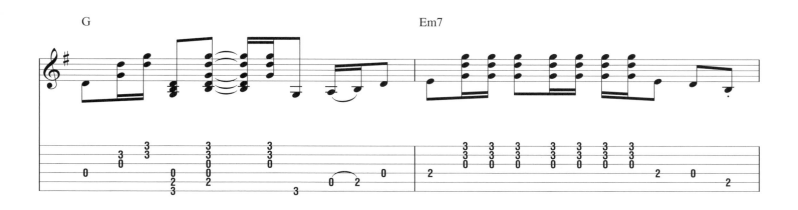

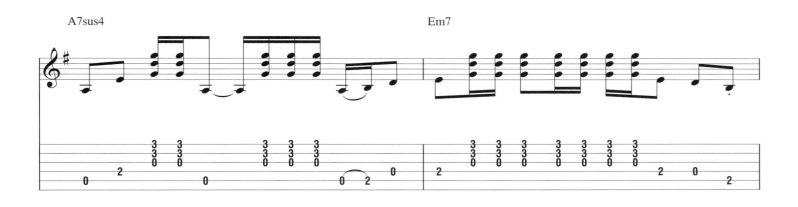

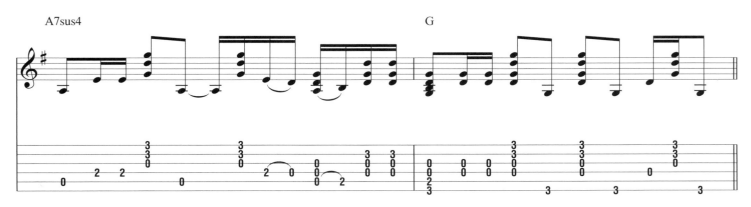

Verse

2. How I wish, ____ how I wish you were here. _____ We're just

*P.M. 6th, 5th & 4th strings, next 7 1/2 meas.

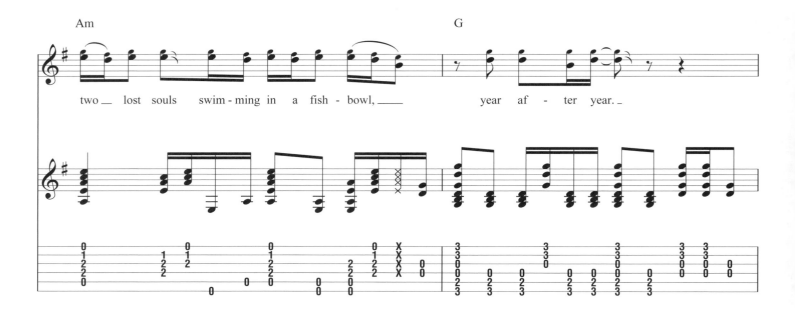

two __ lost souls swim-ming in a fish-bowl, ____ year af-ter year. __

Run-ning o-ver the same __ old __ ground, what have we found? _____ The same __ old __

fears, _____ wish you _____ were here. _____

Outro

Repeat and fade

Run Like Hell

Words and Music by Roger Waters and David Gilmour

Drop D tuning:
(low to high) D-A-D-G-B-E

Intro
Moderately ♩ = 117

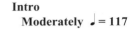

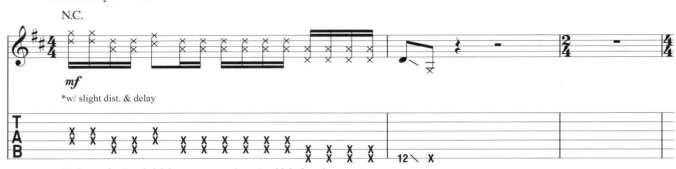

*w/ slight dist. & delay

*Delay set for dotted eighth-note regeneration w/ multiple decaying repeats.

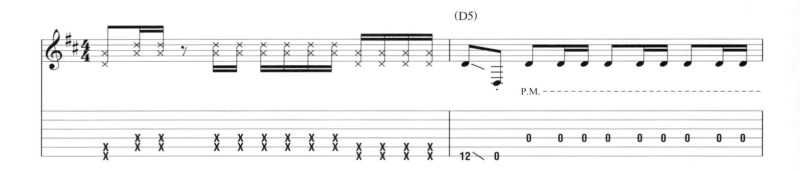

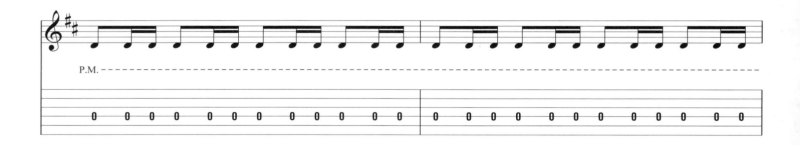

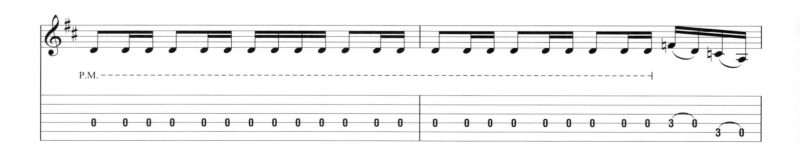

Copyright © 1979 Roger Waters Music Overseas Ltd. and Pink Floyd Music Publishers, Inc.
All Rights for Roger Waters Music Overseas Ltd. Administered by BMG Rights Management (US) LLC
All Rights Reserved   Used by Permission

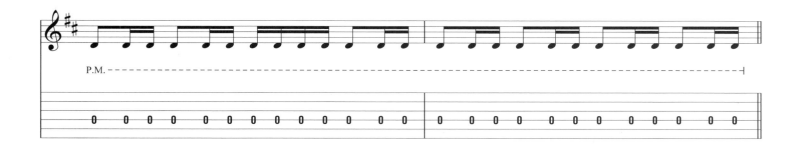

𝄉 Interlude

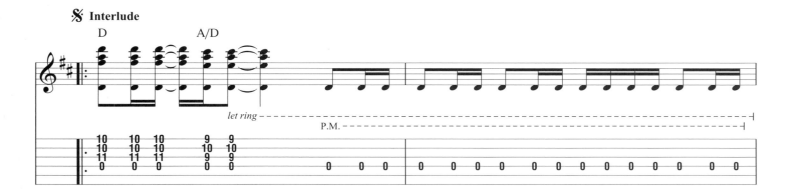

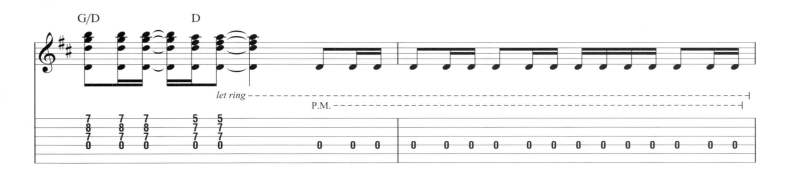

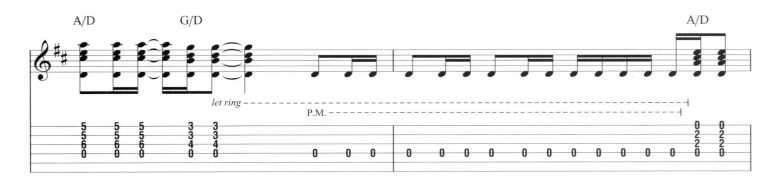

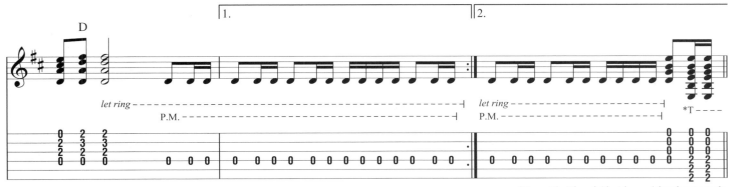

*Barre 4th, 5th and 6th strings w/ thumb over neck.

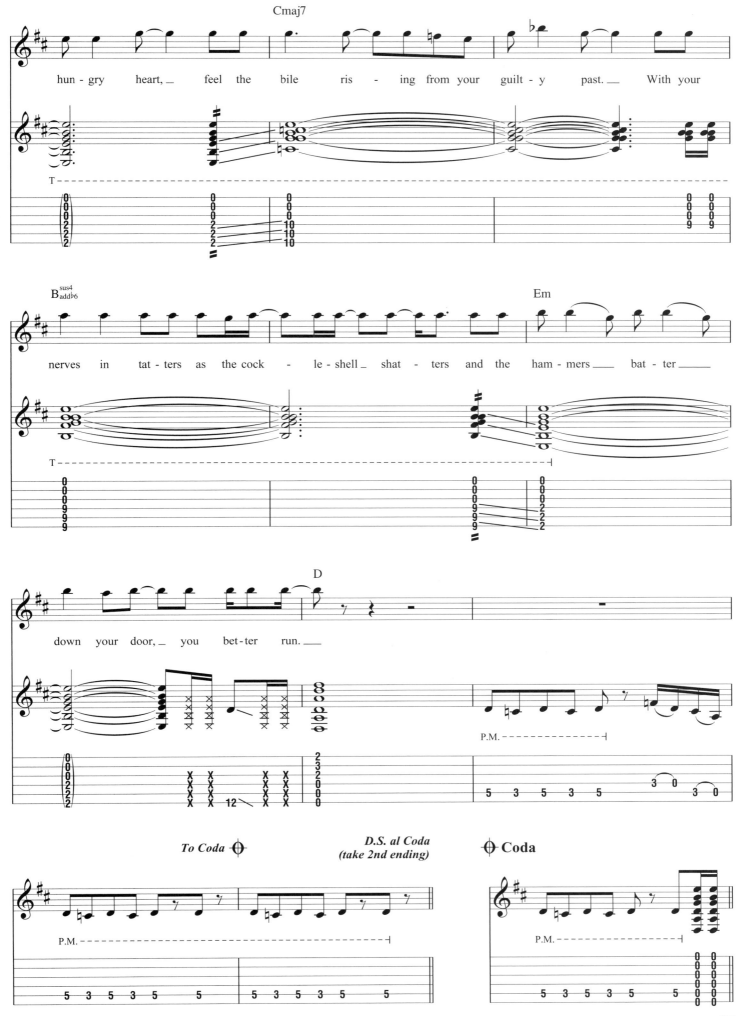

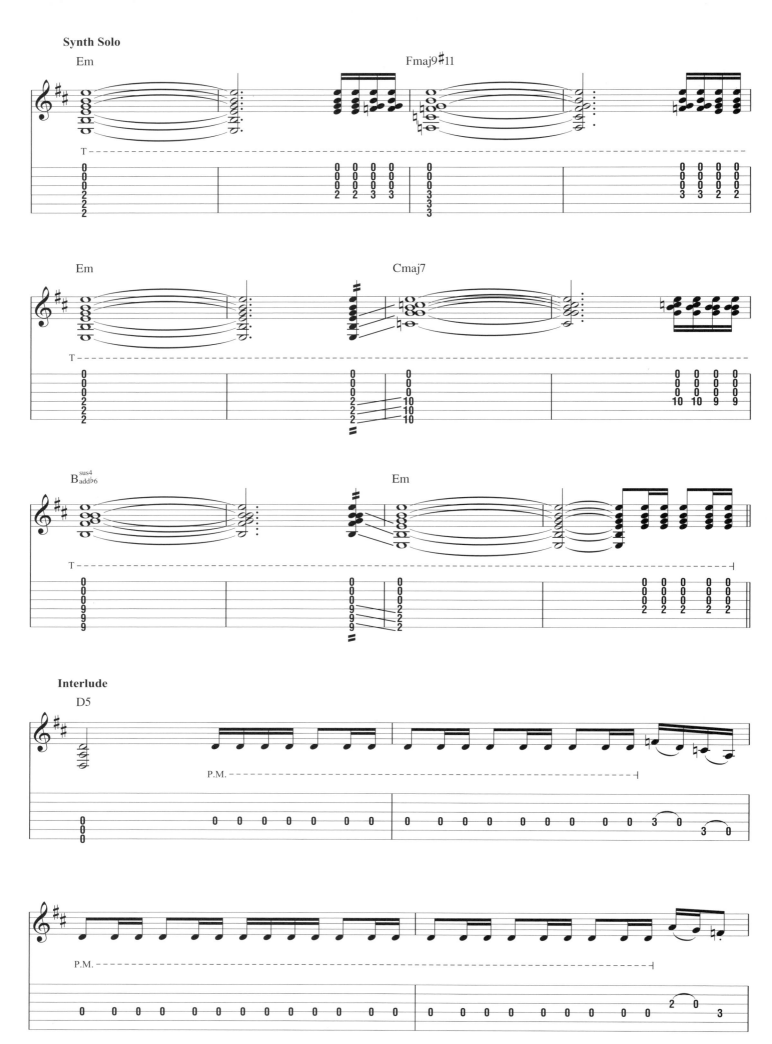

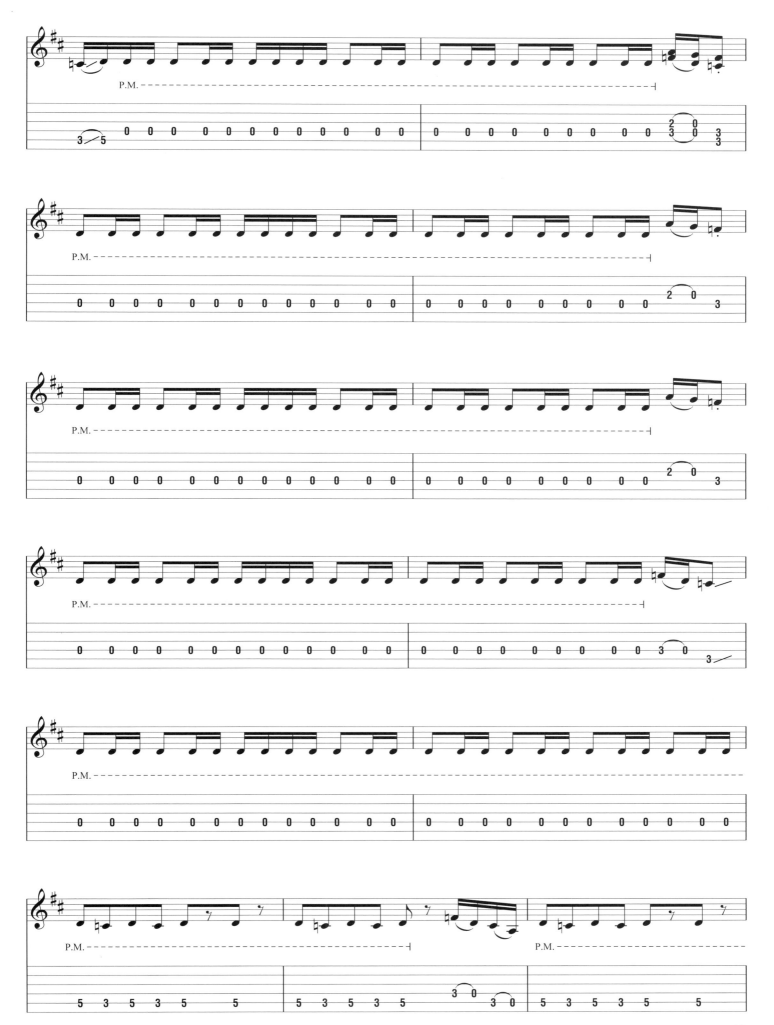

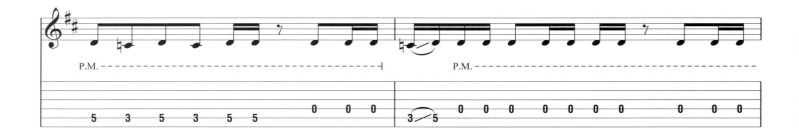

Outro

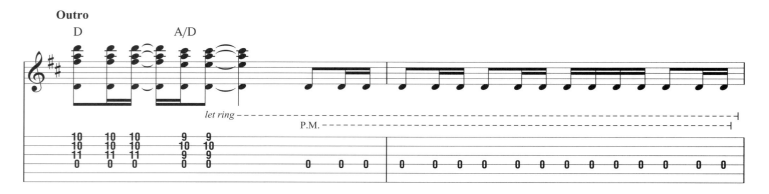

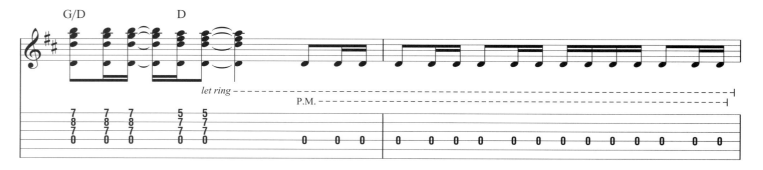

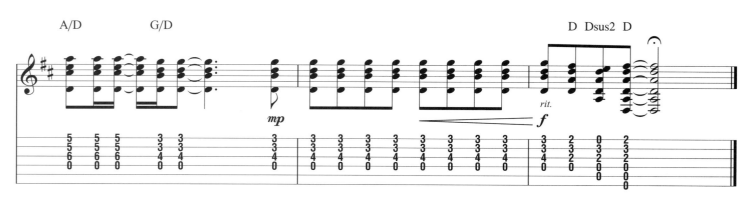

Additional Lyrics

2. You better run all day and run all night, and keep your dirty feelings deep inside.
   And if you're taking your girlfriend out tonight, you'd better park the car well out of sight.
   'Cause if they catch you in the backseat tryin' to pick her locks, they're gonna send you back to mother in a cardboard box.
   You better run.

HAL•LEONARD® GUITAR PLAY-ALONG

AUDIO ACCESS INCLUDED   **INCLUDES TAB**

This series will help you play your favorite songs quickly and easily. Just follow the tab and listen to the CD or online audio to hear how the guitar should sound, and then play along using the separate backing tracks. Playback tools are provided for slowing down the tempo without changing pitch and looping challenging parts. The melody and lyrics are included in the book so that you can sing or simply follow along.

1. ROCK
00699570......................$16.99

2. ACOUSTIC
00699569......................$16.99

3. HARD ROCK
00699573......................$17.99

4. POP/ROCK
00699571......................$16.99

6. '90S ROCK
00699572......................$16.99

7. BLUES
00699575......................$17.99

8. ROCK
00699585......................$16.99

9. EASY ACOUSTIC SONGS
00151708......................$16.99

10. ACOUSTIC
00699586......................$16.95

11. EARLY ROCK
0699579......................$14.95

12. POP/ROCK
00699587......................$14.95

13. FOLK ROCK
00699581......................$15.99

14. BLUES ROCK
00699582......................$16.99

15. R&B
00699583......................$16.99

16. JAZZ
00699584......................$15.95

17. COUNTRY
00699588......................$16.99

18. ACOUSTIC ROCK
00699577......................$15.95

19. SOUL
00699578......................$14.99

20. ROCKABILLY
00699580......................$14.95

21. SANTANA
00174525......................$17.99

22. CHRISTMAS
00699600......................$15.99

23. SURF
00699635......................$15.99

24. ERIC CLAPTON
00699649......................$17.99

25. THE BEATLES
00198265......................$17.99

26. ELVIS PRESLEY
00699643......................$16.99

27. DAVID LEE ROTH
00699645......................$16.95

28. GREG KOCH
00699646......................$16.99

29. BOB SEGER
00699647......................$15.99

30. KISS
00699644......................$16.99

31. CHRISTMAS HITS
00699652......................$14.95

32. THE OFFSPRING
00699653......................$14.95

33. ACOUSTIC CLASSICS
00699656......................$16.95

34. CLASSIC ROCK
00699658......................$17.99

35. HAIR METAL
00699660......................$17.99

36. SOUTHERN ROCK
00699661......................$16.95

37. ACOUSTIC METAL
00699662......................$22.99

38. BLUES
00699663......................$16.95

39. '80S METAL
00699664......................$16.99

40. INCUBUS
00699668......................$17.95

41. ERIC CLAPTON
00699669......................$17.99

42. COVER BAND HITS
00211597......................$16.99

43. LYNYRD SKYNYRD
00699681......................$17.95

44. JAZZ
00699689......................$16.99

45. TV THEMES
00699718......................$14.95

46. MAINSTREAM ROCK
00699722......................$16.95

47. HENDRIX SMASH HITS
00699723......................$19.99

48. AEROSMITH CLASSICS
00699724......................$17.99

49. STEVIE RAY VAUGHAN
00699725......................$17.99

50. VAN HALEN 1978-1984
00110269......................$17.99

51. ALTERNATIVE '90S
00699727......................$14.99

52. FUNK
00699728......................$15.99

53. DISCO
00699729......................$14.99

54. HEAVY METAL
00699730......................$15.99

55. POP METAL
00699731......................$14.95

56. FOO FIGHTERS
00699749......................$15.99

58. BLINK-182
00699772......................$14.95

59. CHET ATKINS
00702347......................$16.99

60. 3 DOORS DOWN
00699774......................$14.95

61. SLIPKNOT
00699775......................$16.99

62. CHRISTMAS CAROLS
00699798......................$12.95

63. CREEDENCE CLEARWATER REVIVAL
00699802......................$16.99

64. OZZY OSBOURNE
00699803......................$17.99

66. THE ROLLING STONES
00699807......................$17.99

67. BLACK SABBATH
00699808......................$16.99

68. PINK FLOYD – DARK SIDE OF THE MOON
00699809......................$16.99

69. ACOUSTIC FAVORITES
00699810......................$16.99

70. OZZY OSBOURNE
00699805......................$16.99

71. CHRISTIAN ROCK
00699824......................$14.95

72. ACOUSTIC '90S
00699827......................$14.95

73. BLUESY ROCK
00699829......................$16.99

74. SIMPLE STRUMMING SONGS
00151706......................$19.99

75. TOM PETTY
00699882......................$16.99

76. COUNTRY HITS
00699884......................$14.95

77. BLUEGRASS
00699910......................$15.99

78. NIRVANA
00700132......................$16.99

79. NEIL YOUNG
00700133......................$24.99

80. ACOUSTIC ANTHOLOGY
00700175......................$19.95

81. ROCK ANTHOLOGY
00700176......................$22.99

82. EASY ROCK SONGS
00700177......................$14.99

83. THREE CHORD SONGS
00700178......................$16.99

84. STEELY DAN
00700200......................$16.99

HAL•LEONARD®

For complete songlists, visit Hal Leonard online at
www.halleonard.com

Prices, contents, and availability subject to change without notice.